Annihilation

by

W.B. Godbey

First Fruits Press
Wilmore,
Kentucky
c2017

Annihilation.
By W.B. Godbey.
First Fruits Press, © 2017

ISBN: 9781621717195 (print), 9781621717201 (digital), 9781621717218 (kindle)

Digital version at http://place.asburyseminary.edu/godbey/2/

Godbey, W. B. (William Baxter), 1833-1920.
    Annihilation / by W.B. Godbey. – Wilmore, KY : First Fruits Press, ©2017.
    43 pages ; cm.
    1. Non sequitur, it does not take place -- 2. Death -- 3. Seventh Day Adventism -- 4. The "day" argument.
    Reprint. Previously published: Greensboro, N.C. : Apostolic Messenger Office, [190-?].
    ISBN: 9781621717195 (pbk.)
    1. Annihilationism. 2. Future punishment. 3. Seventh-Day Adventists--Doctrines. 4. Seventh-Day Adventists--Controversial literature. I. Title.
BT930.G62 2017   236/.23

Cover design by Jon Ramsey

asburyseminary.edu
800.2ASBURY
204 North Lexington Avenue
Wilmore, Kentucky 40390

First Fruits
THE ACADEMIC OPEN PRESS OF ASBURY SEMINARY

First Fruits Press
The Academic Open Press of Asbury Theological Seminary
204 N. Lexington Ave., Wilmore, KY 40390
859-858-2236
first.fruits@asburyseminary.edu
asbury.to/firstfruits

ANNIHILATION

By

W B. Godbey

AUTHOR OF

"New Testament Commentaries." "New Testament Translation," and a great uumber of other books and booklets.

PUBLISHED BY

APOSTOLIC MESSENGER OFFICE

900 SILVER RUN AVE.

GREENSBORO. N. C.

ANNIHILATION

This is the climacteric dogma of the Seventh Day Adventists, prophecied by our Savior and Paul in the last days, as they have no ancient history and are but of yesterday. 2 Tim. 3 chap. Creeping into houses, and leading captive (E. V.) "silly women." The Greek is **gunaikaria,** literally meaning little women as it is the diminutive of **gune,** a woman. As it is neuter gender, it is neither male nor female and therefore includes both, and fully translated, would have to read, silly women and goosey men." Jesus and Paul say that they make them two fold more the children of hell than themselves.

It was originally ascribed to the Scribes and Pharisees, who were exceedingly prosylitic, compassing sea and land to make a prosylite, a convert, a heathen to Judaism. The reason why he would be a two fold child of hell than before was, instead of saving him from the hell of idolatry, they left him incumbered with all of his paganistic abominations and added to that Satanic millstone already around his neck, the abomination of fallen Judaism.

This was hypocrisy in the sight of God, as Jesus constantly called them hypocrites. The meaning of hypocrite is one that plays religion but does not have it. The original word means an actor on the stage, seducingly and magnetically playing an unreal part.

Those Scribes and Pharisees were the Holiness people of the Jewish Church, orthodox and exceedingly punctilious, keeping every ramification of the law. Therefore they had run into dead legalism, cold formality and empty ceremonies, which were awfully stenchy to the divine alfactories, from which He turned away in holy horror. So instead of saving the poor idolater, when they converted him to Judaism, they simply added their own iniquity to the paganistic demonism which he also had.

Chapter I.

NON SEQUITUR, IT DOES NOT TAKE PLACE

There is no such thing in all the world as annihilation, which means to turn something into nothing. The philosophers of all ages have experimented and labored in vain to turn something into nothing. They can destroy it, but that only changes the form. All they can possibly do is to effect a metamorphism.

(a) While preaching in California I found the Seventh Day Adventist's book, "Annihilation," in the mission, left there by some of them for people to read under the positive protest of Brother and Sister Fergurson, proprietors of the mission, who are entirely unwilling for a word of that heresy to get into their mission. They not only slip their books into the Holiness missions, but if not watched and called down, they make "no-hellite" speeches. Therefore it is necessary to keep a constant vigilence over it, or before you are aware, they will actually capture it.

I picked up this book and read it through, and found it the most scriptural I ever saw, containing little comment, but a grand catalogue of quotations, both from the Old and the New Testament. So, an uncultured credulous person would read that book and pronounce it perfectly satisfactory and amen it from beginning to end as they would not dare to contradict God's Word; while at the same time, there was not a single word of truth in it. Among all that grand array of quotations, not one on annihilation, but every one on destruction, which nobody denies and consequently it is not a matter of controversy, but destruction is not annihilation nor akin to it. You can destroy anything and everything you get hold of. Satan, means destroyer, so does "Diabolos," the Latin, "Apolyon," the Greek, "Abaddon," the Hebrew, all mean destroyer, because that is the work of Satan, to destroy all good and transform it into the bad. But destruction never does in any case mean annihilation.

(b) Turn it any way you will. You can destroy it. While I dictate these lines to an amanuensis, I look out on a green tree. It is an easy matter to utterly destroy it, turn it into ashes; trunk, branches, leaves and roots. But if you weigh it after you reduce it all to ashes and gasses, the chemical world has abundantly demonstrated, the perfect equois, they would weigh precisely as much as the tree before it is consumed. Therefore all efforts to annihilate on the line of destruction are an utter failure, demonstrating the truth in which the philosophic world has acquiesed, that nothing at all can be annihilated. It is utterly impossible to turn something into nothing. You can turn it into something else, but it will be a real entity, just as truly as before you tinkered with it.

The principal scripture used by the Annihilationists is the latter part of Malachi, "Behold the day cometh, that shall burn as an oven, when all the gay, all the proud, and all the wicked, shall be stubble, and the Lord of Hosts will burn them up, that there shall be neither root nor branch. But unto you that fear my name, shall the Son of Righteousness arise with healing in His wings, and you shall grow up as calves of the stall, you shall tread down the wicked. They shall be ashes under the soles of your feet, in the day that I shall do thus, saith the Lord of Hosts. Remember ye the Law of Moses my servant, which I commanded unto him in Horeb, with the statutes and judgments. Behold I will send Elijah the prophet before the coming of the great and dreadful day of the Lord and He shall turn the hearts of fathers to the children and the hearts of the children to the fathers, lest I come and smite the earth with a curse." This is the grand battering ram of all the Annihilationists.

(c) Noble saints, have frequently called on me to explain it, as this is the strong citadel, the exegesis for all the balance on that line. All their efforts to prove annihilation do not touch it nor have any reference to it. Satan is wonderful for sham battles, he delights in the **ignis fatnus,** whose delusive ray lights up unreal words and glows but to betray. He delights in fire-works, making grand and magnitudinous exhibitions, when it is like the gossamer that floats in the morning sunbeam evanescing before his accumulated effulgence as he climbs the Orient and floods the world with his noon-day glory.

> "Phaethon, once upon the eternal plain,
> Leaped upon his father's car and seized the rein;
> Far from his track impelled the glowing sun
> Till nature's laws to wild disorder run."

Such is the unhappy fate of people who follow blind guides till they plunge headlong into the unfathomable abyss of irretrivable woe. Everything in the world is Satanic sham and delusion, except God and His truth, which is immutible as is all incommunicable attributes. God is the author of the material world as well as the spiritual. The book of nature reveals God in the former, and the book of grace, the Bible in the latter. Therefore the utter falsity of annihilation.

Long ages rolled away while the infidels throughout the world were making their formidable assaults against the Bible, on the hypothesis of its irreconcilability with the laws of nature. The early explorers of geology held that view, till Hugh Miller, an humble Christian, so utterly refuted them, as he explored the crust of the earth and expounded geology, that reaction took place and the light has been growing brighter ever since the confirmation of the perfect harmony of geology, astronomy and every other science with the precious and infallible Word.

(d) The world is filled with false science as well as false theology. Christian Scientists are taking the world. They are neither scientists nor Christians, because Christianity is all spirituality and they do not believe that you have a spirit. Consequently they have no spirituality. Human science is triconomy because man is a trinity, consisting of spirit (pneuma), soul (psychu) and body (soma). The Christian Scientists teach that man is a diconomy, having only mind and body. Therefore scientifically they are utterly false. Satan is wonderful for good names. When he raised up this denomination, already great and growing with paradoxical rapidity, as it has no cross, he gave it a double name, both really good, but both utterly false in their application to those people, who have neither Christianity nor science.

(e) In that last chapter of Malachi, the Seventh Day Adventists and other annihilationists, get their heavy artilery, "Behold the day cometh which shall burn as an oven and all the wicked shall be stubble, and it will burn them up, saith the Lord of Hosts, that shall neither have root nor branch, but unto you that fear my name, will the Sun of Righteousness arise with healing in His wings; ye shall tread down the wicked, they shall be ashes under the soles of your feet. In the day that I shall do this, saith the Lord of Hosts."

Look at it and see if there is any annihilation in the whole matter. Here the wicked are called stubble and the fires will burn them up, leaving neither root nor branch. And so they say that it is annihilation. That it is destruction, we frankly admit, but what saith the Word: "They shall be ashes under the soles of your feet." Here you see most unquestionably the existence perpetuated in the form of ashes. The stubble is destroyed; it is not straw any more, neither will starving cattle eat it, as they did before it was burnt up, but while it no longer exists in the form of straw, it does exist in the form of ashes, which are as real and substantial as straw, constituting the great fertilizer of the earth. Therefore you see the utter falsity of the annihilation argument.

(f) All this scripture was literally fulfilled in the Jewish Tribulation. Satan had so utterly possessed the higher clergy as to turn them against Jesus at the beginning, because He came into the world in abject poverty and obscurity. Joseph and Mary, though members of the Royal family, in the providence of God, were actually too poor to have a garment for their child to wear when He came into the world. Therefore they picked up old rags, which had been thrown away and sewed them together; thus making the first garment the Savior of the world ever wore. They were too poor to have a lodging. Consequently He had to be born in the calf stable, among the herds and flocks. Herod's soldiers would have surely killed Him if God had not miraculously sent them money from the distant east, by the wise men, who gave Him gold, silver, francincense and myrrh, valuable aromatics, which would command the money, thus defraying that long, expensive journey into Egypt, which was absolutely necessary to save His life.

The Jews blinded and deluded by the demonized high priests and all the influential clergy, had rejected and crucified their Christ, for whom they had waited four thousand years; thus grieving away the

Holy Spirit, crossing the dead line, had become un-savable, plunging into the hopeless idolatry of dead Judaism, having deified and idolized the Mosaic ordi-nances and reached a place where they would have gone on indefinitely through the ages, sacrificing beasts and birds, actually worshipping the symbol-isms after the great antitype had fulfilled all the ceremonial law, bleeding and dying on rugged Cal-vary; all the types and shadows thus fulfilled, nor-mally taking their flight. They had reached an unsavable and incorrigible attitude in which the hope of Israel and the salvation of the world demand-ed their elimination. "He came to His own and His own received Him not, but to as many as received Him, to them gave He the privilege to become the children, who are born, not of blood (sacrifices) nor the will of the flesh (i. e., the carnal will), nor the will of man (i. e., the preacher), but of God." (John 1: 13.) Though our Savior came to His own people, they received Him not with exception of a few poor and influential people. Therefore the rank and file of the nation plunged into idolatry and reprobacy, when mercy to coming generations and the whole Gentile world demanded their removal, the elect few being dispersed to the ends of the earth that they might preserve seed, to receive the fulfillment of the prophecies. While the reprobate Jews became the stubble and were destroyed; in Jerusalem alone, a round million, perishing by the sword, pestilence and famine, during those awful seven years; thus showing the fate of the stubble consumed by the fire.

(g) John the Baptist was Elijah to come. (Matt. 17 ch.; Mark 9 ch.; Luke 9 ch.) A few years ago, the Holiness Movement was all in a puzzle to know which was Elijah, Dowie or Saufred, as they were contesting each other for the crown of Elijahhood, which John the Baptist had been wearing among the angels 1850 years. The great Holiness Movement

simply failing to understand the plain words of Jesus
in the above three chapters and some others. Elijah
was sent into the world to restore the Law in Israel,
which they had so blindly and flagrantly broken.
He labored all his life heroically on that line when
God relieved him with a chariot ride to His own
glorified presence, without ever seeing death; thus
giving us another witness by the side of Enoch, brilliant souvenirs of his original economy, i. e., that
we should all be translated after serving our probation and death would never have thrown his black
shadow over this beautiful Eden world. Four hundred years had rolled away since the days of Malachi,
during which God had not spoken to Israel by human
voice. Dense gloom had settled down on the
whole Hebrew nation; all serious people, profoundly
thoughtful and exceedingly fearful that God had
cast them away to drift on the world-wide sea on
polytheistic idolatry. Therefore the rise of John
the Baptist was really a sunburst on the waning
hope of Israel, as He was not only an inspired prophet, but the greatest that had ever risen. Jesus
said among those born of women, there hath not
risen a greater than John the Baptist; yet the least
in the kingdom of heaven is greater than he.

(h) The Kingdom of Heaven means the Gospel
Dispensation ,which was launched on the Day of
Pentecost, Jesus having come at the end of the Law
Dispensation, "having been born under the law that
He might redeem those under the law." (Gal. 4 ch.)
Thus having by His vicarious, experiatory, substi-
tutionary atonement, prepared all the materials for
the kingdom, launched it on Pentecostal Day by the
baptism of the Holy Ghost and fire, which He gave
His apostles, thus qualifying them to carry it to the
ends of the earth as they did and each one in the
succession of his Master sealed it with his blood.
John the Baptist lived and died under the Law Dis-

pensation, having, like Abraham, Isaac, Jacob, Job
and all the patriarchs and prophets, received sanctification proleptically, i. e., before its time. The weak-
est sanctified disciple of Christ stands on a higher
plane, dispensationally greater than John the Baptist, though the greatest of the prophets. Though
John had been born at Jutta, ten miles from Beth-
lehem, and so far as they knew, in no danger when
the slaughter of the infants was desolating the latter, and indiscriminately in order to make sure of
Jesus, fearing lest they might come to Jutta, his
father and mother had imigrated away to the wilderness of Judah and never came back, thus provi-
dentially bringing up their son among the Essenes,
the poor Holiness people living in the wilderness,
because the land was so cheap and plenty of room.
Consequently John became a hermit prophet. We
see the hermit houses now excavated at the side of
this mountain as we travel through. When he reached majority—thirty years (fifty being maturity)—
responsively to Levitical Law, he began to preach,
already flooded with the Holy Ghost, even from the
womb of his mother. Consequently his messages
were unsheathed lightning, thunder bolts and earth-
quakes, sending panic to every auditor, so they ran
and shouted to everybody they met, "Come and see
the hermit prophet; surely he is the Shiloh and the
Messiah." Consequently all who heard the news
hastened with all expedition to see and hear for
themselves. As the news went on the wings of the
wind, cities were emptied and the people, old and
young, rich and poor, the former on their camels
and the latter trudging through the dust in pedes-
trian multitudes to satisfy their thrilling curiosity,
and see for themselves, if he is not the long-expected
Christ. The multitudes from every corner of the
compass actually thronged the wilderness and necess-
itated the removing of the meeting to the swelling

Jordan, in full view, though twenty miles distance, in order that man and beast may have water to drink as well as for culinary purposes.

(i)   Amid the multitudes at all times may be seen groups of priests with their long rolls of prophecies, straining their eyes to solve the problem whether he is the Christ. Eventually they resolve to settle it by a personal appeal to the hermit prophet of the wilderness, sending a delegation of priests and Levites to publicly interview him, "Art thou the Christ, or do we look for another?" The answer is prompt and unequivocal in the negative. Meanwhile he intensifies their curiosity by the positive assurance that the Christ has already come and he has been sent to introduce Him. Then all hearts are fluttering and eyes wide open to catch a glimpse of Israel's Redeemer and the Savior of the world. The day is bright and fair, and the audience of ten thousand listening to the paradoxical hermit prophet, when suddenly reaching out his hand toward the north star, he shouts aloud, "Behold the Lamb of God that taketh away the sin of the world." (John 1: 29.) All eyes are turned and see a strange young man approaching; the multitudes spontaneously crowding together forming an aisle through which they come to meet each other, as John has dismounted from the great stone upon which he was standing. Now they witness the meeting of the two most important characters ever on the earth, Jesus of Nazareth and the prophet of the wilderness; the former demanding baptism at his hands; the latter, modestly declining, with the apology, "I have need to be baptized of Thee, and comest Thou to me." Then Jesus reminds him, "Suffer it to be so now, as it becometh us to fulfill all righteousness." (Because the Levitical Law required the high priest to be anointed before he enterd upon his office.) Consequently he acquiesced and John pours the limpid rill on the head of his Lord, as we see confered by the statuary, representing Jesus standing and John pouring the water on His head. The house of Judas in Damascus, where Paul was converted and baptized by Annias, is now used as a Greek Church and when I was there again in 1911, I saw in life size statuary, Paul standing and Annias pouring water on his head. We know the baptism of Jesus was His anointing for the High Priesthood, because when He went to Jerusalem and entered upon His priestly office cleansing the temple, driving out the buyers and sellers, the thing which nobody but the high priest had a right to do, and they demanded His authority. He refered them to the baptism of John, showing that He got it there. Therefore John did for Jesus, just what Moses did for Aaron, when he anointed him for the high priesthood, pouring the oil on his head. Again John says that he did to Him with water, the very thing He was going to do to the people with the Holy Ghost and fire. You know, on the Day of Pentecost, the Holy Ghost and Fire fell on the people when Jesus baptized them by pouring. Departure from the truth is always detrimental to spirituality. Two great objections to immersion: one, it is utterly unknown in the Bible and was never seen till every Apostle went to heaven and the people who practice it now, brought it in; the other is that it does away with the baptism of the Holy Ghost, as you see its votaries do not preach nor profess the baptism Jesus gives with the Holy Ghost and Fire, "without which no one shall see the Lord." (Heb. 12: 14.) Baptism has no meaning in the Bible but a purification. The baptism Jesus gives with the Holy Ghost and Fire is your sanctification, the two words being synonomous because Jesus defines **baptidzo** by **catharidzo**, (Luke 11: 38), and **hagiadzo, sanctify,** by the same word. (Eph. 5: 26.)

(j) Satan resorts to myriad devices to becloud the work of Christ by church ordinances or some other phase of idolatry. Nothing in all the universe is necessary to your salvation but Jesus who raises you from the dead in regeneration (John 11 ch.), and baptizes you with the Holy Ghost and Fire. (Matt. 3:11.) John's preaching shook the Hebrew nation from center to circumference, raising all on the tip toe of thrilling anticipation of the Lord's fulfillment of His promises to send the Christ and save them all. John with his transcended eloquence, burning pathos, glowing enthusiasm, preached down from heaven a cyclone conviction on all the people, who in thronging multitudes from dewy morning till dusky eve, hung upon his fire-baptized lips. The result was, revival power shook and revolutionized the homes, fulfilling Malachi's prophecy, "that the second Elijah would turn the hearts of the fathers to the children and the children to the fathers, lest He come and smite the land with a curse." If the people had been true to the preaching of John, that awful curse, the Jewish tribulation, seven years flowing with blood and reaving with flame and heaping the land with the dead. As Josephus says, "During the siege of Jerusalem, they fell dead with the sword, pestilence and famine so rapidly that they could not bury them, so the grim monster stalked through the city like an avenging sceptre, slaying the people in piles." A genuine Holy Ghost revival, such as John's preaching brought, is the very thing to shake the devil out of homes, turning the hearts of the fathers to their children, confessing the neglected duty and begging pardon and the hearts of the children to the parents, confessing their sins, imploring forgiveness and importuning their prayers.

Hence we have Malachi's prophecy fulfilled in the Jewish Tribulation. While Satan got the big end of the battle, as he always will till Christ comes and dethrones him and takes the whole world in hand, so the nation almost unanimously rejected Christ, even after John's wonderful and glorious introductory. But this prophecy was also fulfilled with the few who received Him and to whom He gave power to become the children of God, to whom He said, in his valedictory sermon on Mt. Olivet on Wednesday afternoon, the following Friday, while prophesying the awful judgment coming on His nation; they who fall by the edge of the sword (Luke 21: 24), and be led captive into all nations, at the same time assuring His disciples, "Not a hair of your head shall be hurt," which was literally fulfilled as He miracuously delivered them from the Roman armies after they had finished their work and taken possession. Read that last chapter of Malachi and then read Josephus on the Destruction of Jerusalem and you will find it was all fulfilled; that not a word about the annihilation of the wicked as destruction has any such meaning, ashes being just as real as stubble. So after those "who feared His name" had received the victory treading down the wicked under their feet, they still, in the inspired metaphor, existed in the form of ashes, as while their bodies were alive in the form of stubble. Therefore, out of this forcible symbolism, no honest exigit can get ancitrilla of annihilation.

Chapter II.

DEATH

It has no meaning anywhere but separation from the source of vitality. As God is the life of the universe, material and spiritual worlds all receive their vitality from Him. Flowers bloom, leaves evolve, fruits develop, ripen and are eaten up by animals and revert back to mother earth whence they came. God is the greatest economist in all the universe. He permits nothing to be lost. As He said to the apostles when He fed the hungry multitudes ten or twelve thousand people on five barley loaves and two fishes, and when they had all eaten to perfect satiety, every one a Benjamin's mess, as they were very hungry. Then He charged them, "Gather up the fragments that nothing be lost," and they had at least a hundred times as much food as they had begun with. While His creative power and loving munificence are utterly illimitible, tossing magnitudinous worlds from the tips of His fingers; filling the celestial firmament with blazing suns, revolving planets accompanied by their beautiful satellites, rings and belts and everything throughout these innumerable worlds teems with life, yet there is nothing lost. Every atom of water that God ever created still exists, though undergoing constant mutations, stone, sand, earth, soil, vegetable, animal and infinitively diversified mutations, infinitestimal metamorphisms, constantly going on. Oh, what a history could a particle of dust give us as the ages roll on, cycles come and go. If it could give its history while identified with the great boa constrictor of Africa, a hundred and twenty feet long and the diameter of an ox, during the long life of the monster, then back in the dust again, absorbed by the spungioles of an olive tree, and eaten by a beautiful damsel, having become a constituancy of her organism, moved on the earth, wielded a fossiliferous influence among the people; again back into the animal kingdom and this time having, through the medium of beautiful grass, reached the body of an elephant. So it goes on through ages and cycles. But no annihilation anywhere. Destruction, which the annihilationists erroniously appropriate, is but the transition into another form of existence.

(k) The death of a vegetable of any kind whether the hyssop growing out of the wall of the majestic Cedar of Lebanon, the Greenland fern, growing on an iceberg, or the California Red-wood, fifty feet in diameter, three hundred feet high and six thousand years old; simply means separation from its source of vitality, which is a mere epoch in the divine administration and means no more that your disembarkation from a ship that you may tread terra-firma for a season.

et vice versa. The universe is in constant mutation, God alone enjoying the incomprehensible attribute of immutability. Nothing in the boundless material universe is absolutely **in statu quo**—two successive minutes—as mutation is superscribed on everything in the universe except God, who, in His changeless majesty, purity and glory, abides forever, while everything else in the illimitable universe is **in transitu**—undergoing mutation; what we call destruction being but a name for the infinite diversity of God's vehicles, to keep the infinitesimal machinery of His boundless universe in its normal states, i. e., mutation. It is going on in us while we sleep. If it should cease, it would not effect our existence, but only superinduce a change in the

mode of that existence. While all created entities
undergo these transitions, responsively to the laws
of vitality and chemistry. When existence either
in the animal or vegetable world supervenes, the
vital force is in the ascendancy over the chemical,
till maturity is reached. Then an equilibrium ob-
tains and remains a short time, when the machinery,
undergoes a revolution, the wheels become reversed
and the downward dissolution supervenes with in-
creasing momentum, till the chemical forces achieve
the complete victory over the vital, life evanescing.
Now that entity, whether animal or vegetable, as it
is equally true in the grand realm, both Fauna and
Flora, reversion to the inorganic state supervenes
But that is not the end. Soon nature's car blows
her whistle and vitality mounts the train; in due
time again to disembark and revert to the inorganic
chemical kingdom.

(1) While we see that death in the boundless
universe throughout both of the great vital king-
doms, Fauna and Flora, filling all worlds, burning
deserts and icy mountains, no exception in either
case, the Fauna, whether the magnitudinous elephant
or hippopotomus of the tropics or the white bear or
the reindeer of the icy pools. The banyan tree, with
five thousand trunks, spreading over a lively equa-
torial island are the beautiful ferns, which have
given world-wide celebrity, the icy mountains that
belt the frozen poles, so we actually sing:

> "From Greenland's icy mountains,
> From India's coral strand,
> Where Africa's sunny fountain
> Rolls down the golden strand."

This universal transition from vitality into chemistry, et vice versa, is really the climactric glory of
His wonderful handiwork; nothing in all the universe free from mutation but Himself. The muta-

tion into the vital kingdom cognomined birth; but
into the chemical, called death—simply different
cogs in the majestic wheel of the celestial universe
of whose revolutions there is no cessation, His own
omnipotant hand keeping everything in motion,
beautifully recognized by our Savior's words, "I
work and My Father words."

(m) While this universal and constant endless
chain of metamorphisms characterizes the material
universe, both Fauna and Flora, when we enter the
spiritual realm we see a diametrically opposite defi-
nition of death, which simply means separation from
God, the only source of vitality, while in the material universe it is simply the law of transition, hither
and thither from the vital to chemical, et vice versa.
The reason why these transitions prevail throughout
the Fauna and Flora, into life and out again, is because material entities are constituted of different
elements of which there are sixty-two in the material world—oxygen, hydrogen, nitorgen, carbon, sul-
pher, etc. When the chemical predominates over the
vital, whether in the Fauna or the Flora, these elements forfeit their cohesive power and all separate;
each one standing alone and dropping back to its
place in the chemical world, thus superinducing the
end of the antecedent life.

While that is true throughout the entire material universe, it cannot appertain to the spiritual
world, from the simple fact that every spirit is a unit
and cannot undergo disintegration, i. e., fall to pieces
and forfeit its individual existence like a tree o.
animal, or a human body, undergoes disintigration
when the chemical forces predominate over the vital.
Study this fact carefully as Satan's shrewd prophets
may here get you into the fog. The Seventh Day
Adventists confound life and existence, death and
non-existence; telling us that God alone has life and
immortality, which is true. Consequently they as-

sure you that there is no immortality out of Him,
using that word in the sense of perpetual existence,
which is not true. Satan is the deadest thing in the
universe, the father of death, yet his existence is as
real as that of God and recognized by the same
phraseology. The wicked are all the children of the
devil (John 8: 24), and dead like him, yet they exist
as really and truly as the saints. The very fact that
a spirit is not a complex entity, like a tree or an animal, or a human body, so that it can be disintegrated
each constituent element adverting back to the dust
from whence it came, thus forfeiting its individu-
ality, demonstrates its endless duration. My spirit is
a unit, confirmed by the fact that I can concentrate
my mind on only one thing at a time and is consequently indissoluble. It can be destroyed, as destruction would simply mean the cessation of its
vitality which it only can enjoy while identified
with God, who is our life. During my probation, I
am perfectly free to be true to God and let Him have
His way with me, or deflect from Him and thus
sever my connection with Him. In which case I
am a dead spirit like Satan but shall exist as truly
as glorified Lazarus in Abraham's bosom. Such is
the nature of spiritualities, as to be unsusceptible of
disintegration from the simple fact that there is no
plurality of constituencies to separate either from
other. The will is the king of humanity, and you
know it is a unit. Jesus says, "He who is not against
us is on our side," et vice versa. "No man can serve
two masters." Your immortal soul is a unit and in-
divisible, i. e., either with God or Satan. Therefore
the death of the soul has nothing to do with its existence. With God it is alive; with Satan, dead.
The unity of the human spirit and its indivisibility
constitute an eternal break water against its anni-
hibility, and eternally refuting that seductive heresy

so prominent with Seventh Day Adventists and Russelites.

(n) If the human spirit is susceptible of dying like the body or with it, like all material entities, then our approximations to our death would be always characterized by mental and spiritual debilitation, as in case of the body. It is a well-known fact that this is not true. Richard Watson, author of the Institutes, the great Theologian whose works are studied everywhere, actually dictated those deep and glorious truths while prostrate on a sick bed and approaching the end of life. To the very last, his mind was gigantic, his thoughts brilliant, clear, logical and irrefutable. If the soul died with the body, there would be contemporaneous debilitation manifested every time, which is not true. In countless instances, mentality and especially spiritually, instead of manifesting abatement, actually become more vigorous, demonstrative and even triumphant to the very last, so the exit is not like the sun gradually approaching the western horizon, and finally sinking away and passing into total eclipse, but like the sun in his noonday splendor, evanescing suddenly from his glowing zenith, and leaving the world wrapped in mid-night darkness.

Chapter III.

SEVENTH DAY ADVENTISM

Seventh Day Adventism is really materialistic infidelity. They do not believe you have a soul. They are eroneously cognomened soul-sleepers, which is not true, because they do not believe you have a soul to sleep or do anything else. That is the reason why they are annihilationists. However, they are utterly fallacious, even from a materialistic standpoint because, as we have always shown you, there is no such thing as annihilation in a meterial world, the philosophers, scientists and exegetes of the physical realm, having thoroughly tested and demonstrated, irrefutably, establishing the fact that nothing can be annihilated.

(o) Metamorphism characterizes the entire physical creation. The caterpillar is metamorphosed into the butterfly; after having done his work, spinning his web, wraps himself in his cocoon, to sleep through the long dreary winter, but does not die. All this time he dreams of the oncoming summer, longs to burst his cumbrous shell and sail on butterfly wings in the golden sunlight. But the bright day that sets him free, only accelerates his swift decay. Especially in the Oceanic Fauna, metamorphisms are wonderful and innumerable. While everything in the boundless material realm is constantly undergoing transformation. Nothing at all is annihilated. God is not the author of death. Satan led the way, unfortunately committing suicide, thus becoming the progenitor of death. Having lost his hold on God, severed the umbilical cord through which he received vitality from its only source in the boundless universe, like the ship loosing her moorings, wanders farther into the dreary wilds of the billowy deep, drawn by the succession power of the Seilla on one side and Caribdis on the other, till into one or the other of these roaring whirlpools, down she goes.

(p) When I was a lad, amid the mountains of my nativity, I often saw "shooting stars," as we call them. Midway between Mars and Jupiter, revolve fifty-two small planets, known as the asteroids—believed by the astronomers to have emanated from a large planet in that locality, undergoing explosion and distintegration at some distant day in bygone ages; the larger fragments retaining their orbits and responsively to centripital and centrifugal forces, assuming a spherical shape; still speed their flight through their orbits, whereas the minor fragments were so light that the impetuosity of the explosion carried them away so far as to break the sphericity of their orbits, so they never could get back on their track, but develop into a parabola, which, though running on a circle, never does return to its track, but moves on indefinitely through ethereal space till it reaches the gravity circle of some other planet, in which case it will revolve round it, but constantly approximating it, till gravitation wins the victory over projectility and its falls on it to abide a constituency of it. These meteoric stones have been found in all parts of the world; everywhere identifiable by their constituency of meteoric iron ore.

(q) When Satan, having through illimitable ages sown around the effulgent throne, **primus inter pares,** pre-eminent among his peers, honored with the cognomen, "light bearer," Lucifer; his gigantic intellect conceived the idea of independency, responsively to which he ventured to become a leader; thus calamitously deflecting from God, the only Leader possible in all the universe, as a plurality of leaders

would superinduce confusion, conflict of worlds, crash
of spheres, disharmony, running wild and developing
utter incorrigibility, ultimating in universal wreck-
age and reversion, back to chaos. Every creature in
the universe is a dependant except God. When Lucifer found himself a hopeless drift on the Ocean of
Eternity, he immediately went for company, of which
even misery is fond, superinducing the fatal alloduc-
tion of one-third of the stars, i. e., angels (Rev. 12:
3, 4), ejected from heaven, he made for this newly
born world, on which many believe he had labored
during its fabrication in the service of the Creator
during his archangelhood. As he said to God in Job's
day, responsively to the question, "Why comest thou
into this assembly among the sons of God," "I am
going to and fro in the earth walking up and down
in it." Therefore some have concluded that he was
familiar with it and enjoyed perigrinations hither
and thither, amid the hills and valleys, mountains
and plains. Though I had made three journeys round
the historic world, I had never visited the land of Uz
for the want of a rail road. When the Lord permit-
ted me to make my fourth tour in 1911, I was delighted to find they had built a railroad from Haiffa Palestine by the Sea of Galilee, eastward through the
ancient land of Bashan, the Kingdom of Og into the
land of Uz, which I found a delectable plain, envir-
oned by the mountains and exceedingly fertile and
beautiful as I might have inferred, because in Job's
day there were so few people in the world and they
had pick and choice of the whole earth and consequently only used the most fertile regions.

(r) As above observed, the Seventh Day Adventists do not believe you have a soul. As a people,
they have no ancient history, as they are but of yesterday. When they sprang up they were very ag-
gressive and itinerary, astonishing the Orthodox
Churches by their new and strange doctrines.

Forty years ago a shrewd, tall, brilliant preacher came from New York into central Kentucky to the cross-road village and began to preach in a church built by Methodists and Campbellites. He was powerful on the coming of the Lord, the renewal of the earth, and its inheritance for the saints—all of which we gladly accept, much enjoy and constantly preach. At the same time, with thrilling emphasis, he poured condemnation on the First Day Sabbath of Christendom, pronouncing it a dangerous heresy and forcing his Old Testament arguments for the Seventh Day with irrefutable, Herculean logic and challenging all the preachers to debate with him. I was in a remote part of the conference, cultivating the field, the Presiding Elder had assigned me, when I received a letter urging me to accept his challenges and debate with him. They were utterly new in the State, as well as elsewhere, scattered wildly from ocean to ocean in their paridoxical aggressiveness. I accepted the challenge, boarded a steam-boat, as railroads were few, came down to Cincinnati and ransacked the book-stores, fortunately found books setting forth their doctrines. The arrangement to begin Tuesday morning and run till Saturday morning—traveling on Monday and using the five days in the debate. As I had recently had a number of debates with Campbellites, I was well up to the business. The forensic discussion is recognized in logic and provided for. It runs very nicely; each contestant chooses his moderator to stand by him in the debate and see that he gets his rights, i. e., equal time, affirming and responding alternately. Meanwhile they were to choose a third man to serve as umpire, take charge of the discussion, call out the speakers, call them down when their time expires, keep order in the congregation and decide all points of controversy in which the moderators do not agree.

(s) I chose an old Methodist preacher to serve as my moderator. As his church was utterly new and he had no preacher, he selected the old class-leader of the Methodist Church, whom with the big end of the membership, he had succeeded in prosely-ting to Seventh Day Adventism along with the larger hemisphere of Campbellism. Both of these churches had an organization in the house,and his denomination became the third. When we opened the debate, I affirmed the souls immortality two solid days to a crowded house, many without who could only hear through the doors and windows; himself denying it and positively unifying the soul and body, ridiculing the idea that you have any soul separate from your body. In his powerful speeches, standing before the multitude, stretching up toward the ceiling, vociferating, "Gentlemen and ladies, you see a soul standing before you six feet tall." The people were surprised beyond all utterance as they took it for granted that he believed in the soul's immortality. The third day brought round his turn to wield the laboring oar. Shouldering the **onus probandi**—burden of proof—he proceeded to affirm the doctrine of his church appertaining to the supernatural birth, the pillow of Bible Theology, the anchor of the Christian's hope, the **sine qua non** of every soul, i. e., the thing every one is obliged to have. His affirmation read, "The supernatural birth (John 3 ch.) will take place on the resurrection morn. As we have no soul to be regenerated, and possess nothing, but this body; when it dies it will sleep in the grave till the resurrection trumpet shall awake it, when it will rise and live again. This will be the new birth and all there is of if and pertinent only to the saints, while the wicked will never rise again, but die like swine, go back to the dust whence they came and be nothing through all eternity." The battle waxed hot; we got into close quarters; swords crossing and fire flashing.

The man found the debate no child's play, as it could just not hold anything; everything being wrested out of his hands, leaving him nothing at all. The crowd was very large and listened spell-bound. The man actually humiliated himself by begging leniency, which I could not give him for the Truth was at stake and the destiny of souls hanging on the issue. I said to him face to face, "You brought this debate on yourself, challenging every preacher that came along. Therefore, you can blame nobody but yourself. The day of mercy is past; your head has to come off. It is heretical. Therefore the two-edged, New Jerusalem blade (Heb. 4: 12), will cut it off, leaving neither distinction nor mercy."

(t) Then I proceeded to give them God's Word: 2 John, "If any one shall come to you, not bearing this doctrine, (i. e., the soul's immortality, salvation by grace, endless life for the righteous, and eternity of woe for the wicked), ye shall not receive him into your houses, nor bid him God speed." This man came to you a long way, a total stranger, and instead of bringing these grand wholesome irrefutable Bible truths on which the Lord has built His Church and against which the gates of hell will never prevail, he has brought heresy. You have received him into your house and bidden him God speed, though he does not so much as believe in the soul's immortality—worse than a heathen for they all do believe in it.

For some time I had observed that the old class-leader, his moderator, was dying by inches. Therefore when I reached that grand logical culmination, saying to them, "God will put me on the witness box at the Judgment day to testify against you all, because you have received this infidel into your house and bidden him God speed." That moment he fell from his chair, down on his knees, crying aloud, "Brethren, I can stand this thing no longer; you must pray for me. Others fell all round, crying for mercy and we had to turn the debate into a revival to get them all reclaimed. The result was they all dropped him like a hot potato and came back into the Methodist Church. The Campbellites received so much fire that it burnt up the water and they gave up their organization. Seventh Day Adventism actually evanesced out of the country though he had several other little churches started, and the work was growing rapidly and spreading out of the country. He left and never came back and his work was blown away by the zephyrs of truth and righteousness and that country is the most incontaminated by that heresy I know in all my travels which are more extensive than those of any other man you ever saw.

(u) Though I did not live there at that time, it so happened in the providence of God that my dear wife was born and reared at Perryville, only seven miles from that place.

When the Holiness Movement crossed the Ohio River at Cincinnati thirty years ago, our presiding Bishop McFyere, a Holiness man, solidly Wesleyan, that tended our convention, welcomed the movement into Dixie Land, took me out of my conference, and **per se,** as there was no evangelistic opportunity, put me in the work, giving me the whole connection for my field of labor, and I have been in it ever since. As that appointment took me from home for life to be a sojourner upon the face of the earth for Jesus' sake, leaving my family, to meet them on the bright, shining shore, where sickness, sorrow, pain and death are felt no more, where the wicked cease from troubling and the weary are forever at rest. Feeling assured that my dear wife left alone, would be happier in her native land, among her consanguinity and the friends of her childhood, going thither I settled for life. Consequently in my visits home I perpetuate a better acquaintance with that country than any other and if there is a Seventh Day Adventist in forty miles I would have no idea where to find him.   I took the Word of the Lord and exposed their bleak and unapplausive infidelity, till the people all saw it; dropped it apparently forever, as burnt children always dread the fire and quit playing with it.

Chapter IV.

THE "DAY" ARGUMENT

This is the lasso which the rangers toss so adroitly as they run over the country, catching the unweary right and left, old and young, great and small and hauling them in.

Nearly forty years ago I was in a glorious revival far out on the Mexican border, where half the population are barbaric Mexicans and the balance wild border ruffians. I had found a favorite place for recreation among the muskeet trees, beautiful evergreens, as it was far down on the Mexican border where summer ever comes and winter never comes, flowers never fade and fruits never fail, with their mid-winter actually hot and dusty like summer; unexpectedly a person walked up to me and said, "You had better get away from here as you are not aware of the danger that you are in. A stranger stopping with us a few days ago, was walking under the lovely shade of the trees which you are now enjoying, when suddenly a lasso dropped over his head, catching him around the waist, enclosing his arms so he could not do anything and the other end attached to a wild horse, mounted by a robber and suddenly dragged the man a hundred yards, almost killing him, till he entered a comatose state, in which he remained while the robber spoliated him. Then mounting his horse he galloped away, making his escape with all the man's money and other things which he thought worth taking; thus leaving him to die. I took the warning and retired from my favorite recreation ground under those lovely trees to return no more. I mentioned this to illustrate with what adroitness these people lasso the innocent.

(v) Early in the Holiness Movement in a Kentucky town of five hundred, we had a wonderful meeting, running almost a year and spreading Holiness far and wide over the country; so we organized the Green River Holiness Association of a thousand members. During that wonderful revival, a beautiful, bright and charming young lady, a Campbellite, had been brought up to believe that she was a Christian because she joined the church and was immersed for the remission of sins. She saw the Christians crowd the altar, linger and pray; arise with radiant faces, telling to all around, the wonderful Sanctifier they had found. She thus solilliquised, "I have long thought that a Christian needed something else and now I see what it is. It is sanctification." Therefore, having no doubt that she was a Christian, she goes to the altar, the saints pray and instruct her. Eventually rising, she shouts like an angel, telling them all she has got it and is gloriously sanctified. Of course the spiritual people all thought that she had just been converted, as Campbellism doesn't give its votaries anything but church-joining, just like joining a lodge, but no one said anything. The meeting ran not only weeks, but months, about a year, I think. Eventually she sees, as the light shines into the heart, the sin personality hiding there in the bullrushes of depravity and gets convicted for sanctification sure enough, now thoroughly convinced that the former was simply regeneration. Therefore, coming to the altar again, she lingers quite awhile. Finally a regular heavenly landslide hits her soul and she rises with shouts of victory. By this time her church has become so disgusted with her, thinking that she has gone into wild fanaticism, that they drop her like a hot potato. No Holiness Churches then had been organized.

Therefore she comes at once and joins the Methodist.

(w) I had written my "Women Preacher," and
the Lord was wonderfully using it to disfranchise
the daughters of Jerusalem, who were hearing the
call to preach through the heavenly vision, consequently she got to preaching with the Holy Ghost
sent down from heaven and was anxious for a field
of labor. I wrote to our missionary board at Nash-
ville, Tenn., recommending her for the foreign field.
They gave her work among the wild Indians in the
territory now the great state of Oklahoma.   There
the Lord wonderfully blessed her ministry and she
was delighted to preach the Gospel sent down from
heaven. Finally a Seventh Day Adventist came along
and at the single toss of the lasso, captured the poor
thing. When the news reached the missionary board
that she had turned Seventh Day Adventist, they
took her work from her. They did her as they do all
the balance—caught her with the "Day" lasso and
then proceeded to lead her into their infidelity and
convince her that she was a sister to the hill frog.
Though they did not quite succeed, they got her as
blue as indego, her happy experience of regeneration
and sanctification having gone into an awful eclipse.
As she had lost her work, she returned home, dying
with the blues. I went back to Robards where she
had been saved and sanctified and found her in the
awful dilema, lassoed by those heretics and Satan,
not only playing the vampire sucking her blood all
out, but actually picking her bones. I told her, to
make a short story of it, that she had made the mis-
take of her life, permitting those heretics getting
their Satanic lasso around her neck and getting her
back into the Slough of Despond, for the last hope
was actually bidding her an eternal adieu. Therefore
I tell her that that altar is her place again and not to
bother herself but cut the matter short in righteousness and go down to the bottom and turn the matter

over to the Lord, as His grace is more than a match
for the devil with all his power of Sabbatic argument,
which she could not answer and over which she had
stumbled and fell head long into the quay of lugu-
brious apostacy. She took me at my word, went to
the bottom, abanded every thing and the Lord wonderfully blessed her and restored, so the shout came
back in jubilant raptures. Yet amid her shouts, her
tears of sorrow were mingled with the efussions of
joy, because she had lost her work. I said to her,
"Dry up your tears, I can get your work back." Then
I wrote to the board, stating the whole matter, how
these heretics had lassoed her and she had been in-
nocently captured and how she had been reclaimed
and was all right again but broken-hearted because
she had lost her work. They simply wrote me that
they were broken-hearted too, as they could not use
a Seventh Day Adventist, opening the door for Satan
to capture it, the world without end, and as she was
restored they were only so glad to take her back and
give her work. Therefore she again went away with
a shout, telling her friends she was going to have
some sense the balance of her life and not get lassoed.
That is the great trouble, so many get caught in
Satan's lasso. For this reason they need my book
and others on Holiness unto the Lord, to fortify
them against Satan's mighty serpentine lasso.

(x) The Seventh Day Adventists tell us that
the Apostolic Church kept the seventh day without
a break till the pope changed it to the first. Not a
word of truth in it, as there never was a pope till the
seventh century to do anything and history, both
sacred and secular, certifies that the first day of the
week was kept from the resurrection of our Lord, as
a sacred memorial Sabbath. (Acts 20: 7; 1 Cor. 16:
2.) The same we have in Roman history of the
early centuries of the Christian era, Sallus, Seuton-
ius, Pliny, Livi, and Juvenal. These historians were

all heathen, in full sympathy with the government and its efforts to eliminate Christianity from the globe. Describing it, among all other events in their day and time, they write it up as a strange heresy, which broke out in Palestine, during the proconsulship of Pontius Pilot, and the reign of Tiberius Caesar and that it was so antagonistic to the Roman gods, under whose auspices they had conquered the world and established the empire, that it was justly condemned under the double charge of high treason against the government and heresy against all their gods, both of which were capital crimes. Consequently the emperors did everything in their power to stop the spread of it. They said that the great trouble in the case was that its votaries had the power to transmit it **volens nolens,** willing or unwilling. Consequently it was very dangerous to handle them and enforce the law against them, because they could transmit it to you **volens nolens.** Consequently while they were prosecuting them they would get it and then they would have to kill them. [You see the solution of the whole problem; the Christians shouted and testified so while they handled them that even the officers would get converted and then they would have to kill them.] Consequently they made short work in every case of prosecution, lest they might catch it and lose their lives, which would necessarily follow in every case. Therefore they would arrest them on suspicion and bring them before the criminal court, and make short work of it: ask them only one question: **"Domicinum servasti?"** "Hast thou kept the Lord's day?" He would answer, **"Christinus sum, intermittere non possum."** "I am a Christian and cannot omit it." Then they would proceed, either to cast him to a wild beast or burn him or kill him some way without delay.

(y) The very fact that they never did ask him:

"Sabbaticum Servasti." "Hast thou kept the Sabbath?" is positive proof they were not keeping the seventh day of the week; which was never called the Lord's day, but simply the Sabbath. These historians give us a cloud of irrefutable testimony, indisputable because its from our enemies, who, of course would not confess judgment against themselves but do their best to defend their own cause. The first Christians were all Jews. In less than a century, the Church underwent a complete change and became all Gentile. The last we see of the Jewish wing of the Church was A. D. 73, when the disciples, having survived the destruction of Jerusalem, fled to Pella in De Capolis—a Gentile kingdom frequently mentioned in the New Testament, bordering on the east bank of the Galilean sea. Our Savior went thither (Luke 8 ch.) on an evangelistic tour: meanwhile the legion hermit was gloriously converted; the legion of demons ejected and entered into the swine. When he got converted he wanted to go with Jesus and preach, but as the apostles were all Jews and Jesus Himself a Jew, He answered him in the negative: the Gospel having not yet been given to the Gentiles, but honored him with a big appointment, giving him all De Capolis, the ten cities for his field of labor. Going to which he preached heroically, as the record says, "All over them." History certifies to his great success, especially at Pella, the most southern city, and hence most convenient for Hebrew refuges, as the imperial edict, under which it was destroyed, made it a penalty of death for a Jew to be found anywhere in the Holy Land, or in any other country under heaven, travelling with his face toward Jerusalem. He was to be taken up and killed, when miracuously rescued from the awful doom which came upon their unbelieving consanguinity; they escaped out of the city, and the Roman armies captured it. They fled away through the wilderness, crossed the Jordan and trending north, came to Pella, there felicitously finding a great number of happy Gentile Christians, who met them with shouts of victory, took them in their arms and bade them welcome to their happy and peaceful homes and a place by their side as they go out to press the conquest to the ends of the earth till their risen and glorified Captain shall return with His mighty angels to dethrone Satan and reign forever.

This was the last of the Jewish wing of the Gospel Church, absorbed with the Gentiles, before the close of the first century, and consequently the last anybody in the Christian Church keeping the seventh day, as the Hebrew Christians kept both Sabbaths, the first and the seventh days as long as they lived. Whereas the Gentile Christians kept only the first day and were not required to keep the seventh as you see in the Jerusalem council, (Acts 15 ch.) where it is not laid down in its specification, but they were only required to abstain from idolatry and from eating blood, (common among the heathen), and animals choked to death and consequently the blood in them, thus giving two specifications on the blood as that is the great item by which we are saved and sanctified and have the victory forever. They are also required to abstain from fornication: the emphasis being on the spiritual and not simply the physical and consequently negatively envolving entire sanctification, as in this way we get married to the Lord, all carnal lovers, i. e., spiritual fornication being discarded.

(z) At Jerusalem we have six Sabbaths every week. We have many Christians there now: a large interesting, and flourishing American colony. Also a very large German colony, French, English, Italian and others. If I were young I would go to the missionary field and spend my life; Jerusalem by choice,

yet not my own will but His. Because Sabbath is
the best day for preaching and at Jerusalem I would
have six every week. Sunday I would preach to
the Christians; Monday to the howling Dervishes, so
called because they howl in their meetings like dogs
and wolves; Tuesday to the Jumping Dervishes, as
that is their day and they are so called because they
jump like Burning Bush people and jump till they
wear out and fall in their tracks; Wednesday I could
transact all my business as nobody keeps that for
a Sabbath; Thursday I could preach to the regular
Dervishes as that is their day; Friday to the Mo-
hammedans, the popular church of the whole country, i. e., the government church; Saturday of course
I would preach to the Jews, who have so gathered
from the ends of the earth as to have the majority
in Jerusalem.

(p) The change of days was made from the
resurrection of the Lord and is really a simple homo-
genius of the genius of our dispensation. . The law
says, "Do your work and then rest and if you do not
finish your work you shall not rest," while the Gospel says, "Rest first and then do your work," as a
well rested man will do so much more work than a
tired man. The law says, "Pay me what you owe
me"; the Gospel says, "I will freely forgive you all
and only ask you to be true to God and meet me in
heaven." Therefore you see the change was super-
induced by the very genius of the dispensation. If
I lived among the Seventh Day Adventists or Jews
I would keep that day and go to their meeting and
lovingly invite them to come to my meeting the next
day. As you see at Jerusalem there are six Sabbaths every week, therefore "let every one be fully
persuaded in his own mind." (1 Cor. 8 ch.) In this
chapter and Romans 14 chapter, Paul loosedly ex-
pounds the whole problem so we can all see it in his
exegesis of food and days, as all the meat salted was
sacrificed to some of the heathen gods. Paul said if

they had clear light and could see that the idol was nothing at all and it did not hurt the meat to sacrifice to it, they could go ahead and eat as much as they pleased, but if they hadn't the full light so they could see when they were eating the meat they were worshiping the idol, they would have to let it alone and the same way about the day. One man regardeth one day above another and another one every day alike. So let every one be fully persuaded in his own mind. If you believe that the seventh day is the correct one, go ahead and keep it and don't fail because if you do not your own conscience will condemn you and you must have a conscience void of offence toward God and man; yet in that case, though you keep the seventh day, you must keep the first day also, because 550 millions of Christians believe Sunday is the correct day and keep it, therefore if you don't keep Sunday holy, you will sin against their conscience and Paul says, "When you so sin against the brethren and wound the weak, (weak because they think you are desecrating the Sabbath when you are not), you sin against Christ; whereas the Seventh Day Adventists have a terrible ordeal if they work on Sunday because they sin against 550 million of Christians and in so doing sin against Christ and consequently their consciences are guilty and they are under condemnation and lose their souls. If you have a conscience for some other day, you must keep that day or you will be convinced at the tribune of your own conscience, while at the same time all the people in the world must form the simple fact that 550 million of Christians keep it and if you desecrate it you sin against the consciences of that mighty host and Paul says, (1 Cor 12 ch.), "When you sin so against the brethren you sin against Christ.

God bless you all!

W. B. GODBEY.

www.ingramcontent.com/pod-product-compliance
Lightning Source LLC
Chambersburg PA
CBHW030309030426
42337CB00012B/647